HOW TO WRITE A NOVEL

In Seven Easy Steps

BY

PROFESSOR ALAN DALE DICKINSON

This book is a self-help book and not a work of fiction. Without limiting the rights under the copyrights of the United States of America, no part of this publication may be reproduced, stored in or introduced into a retrieval system, or transmitted, in any form whatsoever, or by any means (electronic, mechanical, photocopying, recording, or otherwise), *without the prior written permission of both the copyright owner and the publisher/author of this said book.*

The scanning, uploading, and distribution of this book via the Internet, or via any other means without the permission of the author, owner, is illegal and also is punishable by law. Please purchase only authorized electronic editions, and do not participate in or encourage electronic piracy of legally copyrighted materials. Your support of the author, co-publisher and owner's rights is greatly appreciated.

Copyright © 2013 (Republished 2021) by Professor Alan Dale Dickinson

All rights reserved, including the right of reproduction in whole, and or in part, and in any such form whatsoever.

ISBN: 978-1-7361464-2-2

DICKINSON, PROFESSOR ALAN DALE
HOW TO WRITE A NOVEL
Dickinson Publishing Company
Professor Alan Dale Dickinson
Chairman and Chief Executive Officer and,
Bank of America
Vice President and Business Banking Manager
World Corporate Lending Group (Retired)
P.O. Box 3962
Laguna Hills, CA 92654

DEDICATION

To Lynn, the love of my life, my most precious, and exquisite, and lovely bride.

This book, *How to Write a Novel*, is dedicated to my beloved granddaughter Morgan Marie, who sings, acts, is very creative, artistic and personable, who is quite capable to becoming anything in her life she wishes to do. Also, to my intelligent son, David Alan and his wife Desiree', and her parents Cesar and Yolanda.

And, Betty Jarvis, my wonderful adopted mother. She is the reason that I am still able to write my novels and books. She is the most dear and precious person in my whole life. Indeed. Also, her great children, Doug and Pam, Ginger and Mark.

 Also, my good personal friends. Brother Thomas and Pamela, Mary, Carol, and my sister-in-law's, Jan, husband John, and Lisa, husband Bob. And my beloved mother-in-law, Jan. Also, Juanita, Janey, Gary, Betty, Diane, and Mr. Brad Hudson, Catherine and Teresa.

With my smart cousin Lee, Inge and his whole family. Dr. Anne, DC Brett Long, with long time friends, Wayne and Donna Leicht in lovely Laguna Beach.

And, last however certainly not least, my humble 'Thank you' to all of you out there on your Kindles, notebooks, lap tops, desk computers, on-line, or in book stores. And, also my sincere apolo-

PROFESSOR ALAN DALE DICKINSON

gies to anyone who I may have accidentally forgotten to acknowledge in this section of my book that I should have.

TABLE OF CONTENTS

PROLOGUE 1

ONE—Pick your Topic 5

TWO—Manuscripts and Citations 14

THREE—Select your Format 27

FOUR—Margins and Copyrights 38

FIVE—Length and Pricing 47

SIX—Editing is your Key 56

SEVEN—Select your Publishing Mode 66

EPILOGUE 75

PROLOGUE

People ask me all of the time, "Alan, where do you get your ideas for all of your crime-fiction mystery novels?" And after much thought, this is what I came up with to respond to them. I have always had an overactive imagination, ever since I was a little kid.

Now, all I do is "open the barn door to my little brain, and let the horses out, and then let them run wild with my imagination." That is the best answer that I could come up with, so I hope it works for my good readers.

Am I writing this self-help book, "How to Write a Novel" because I am the world's foremost author? Or since I am a New York Times bestselling writer? Or due to the fact that I am a perfect speller? Or that I am a great grammar guru? No, no, no and no again.

The plain and simple explanation why I wrote this book is to assist, and make it easier for new, first time authors to start and complete their first novel. Also, to save them months, or even years, to accomplish their 'life time goal' to write their book, finally. There are lots, and lots, of sources for new authors to get help with their desire to write their literary Master Piece.

This is just one, small, *life raft* in the 'sea' of novel writing suggestions. Please accept it as such, and I sincerely hope, that it will assist you, a lot, and if not, I can absolutely guarantee you that none of the aforementioned suggestions will hurt your novel project.

I have heard sports enthusiasts say that a lot of very good coaches, often were not great players, when they played their respective sports. Having said that, some think this is also true as well of authors who write self-help books like, "How to Write a Novel." Perhaps, I will be able to produce a great 'How to...' book even though I am clearly (in my opinion), not a great author. Just saying.

Now, at this early point in time, and prior to your reading my book, I feel a 'disclaimer' is in order as well as very necessary. I realize that part of the title of my book is, "In Seven Easy Steps." Well yes, the writing of your first novel or book, will be much easier after you read this little self-help book. I must tell you, however, that yes, I am convinced that it will be easier, yes, much easier, albeit, not 'easy'.

As in easy and that it will not take a great deal of hard work, very hard work, long hours and lots of time and effort on your part. Your novel is not going to write itself and no one can write it for you. You will get Writers Block sometimes, however, that is alright and you just have to work through that. All authors get that, so please do not feel distraught and give up on your dream of becoming an author.

I must also confess to you good readers out there that I (this said author), love the Esoteric *and* Artful things in the crazy, old, mixed up world that we find ourselves living in today. And, I thoroughly enjoy playing with the Kings English, or our version of it, anyway. Also, I like to 'wax and wane' *philosophically* about a variety of subject matters, and sometimes, just once in a while, they are a little bit off point.

I hope that you readers will understand that slight writer's flaw. Some have called me a Literary *Iconoclast* (an author who deviates from the normal writing establishment). And also, one whom writes on an *Eclectic* range of subject matters and /or topics. (Please see his Amazon internet site). And some said that "Dickinson is a very interesting as well as very well-educated author."

Finally, to complete my Introduction, I respectfully request that you good readers not be too overly critical of any typo's, spelling or grammar (composition), errors in this little self-help book. Please recall that I am a: Accounting, Economic, Finance, Management, Real Estate, and Marketing major.

Also, please remember that it is written simply to assist you with the writing of your first, and, simple novel. Period. It is not meant to be a literary Master Piece, yet, hopefully *yours* will be. If you are a good writer of English articles, letters, emails, blogs, or you have already done some research and/or written a book already, then this book, "How to Write a Novel" may not be of a lot of help to you, perhaps.

If you purchase it, you can just 'scan' it quickly and 'glean' from it some points that you did not already know, if any, of course. Then you can give it to someone whom you know who is not as adept at writing as yourself, or simply return it. It's your call, of course.

For your *information*, I have written, edited, and published and/or co-published Twenty-Seven (27) novels/short stories/novellas /self-help books, in paperback form. I also have Twenty-three (23) eBooks listed on Kindle for sale. My novels, et cetera, are available for purchase In twelve (12) foreign countries. Including the following:

Canada, Mexico, Brazil, Germany, France, Spain, Italy, India, UK (England), Australia, as well as Japan.

Just one last point by this said author, if you will allow me, I am not a literary agent, or copyright attorney, nor a lawyer of any kind. You should protect yourself as well as the rights of ownership (copyrights), by seeking the assistance of a good contract (author agreement) as well as a respected copyright attorney. Even if you find a regular publisher, you should do this, remember they are in business to make money not protect *your* rights. Indeed.

CHAPTER ONE
PICK YOUR TOPIC

The information in this little self-help book on **How to Write a Novel**, took me four years to learn. If you do not already know this crucial material, or you were not an English nor Journalism major at your University, or you were not able to afford to go to College, et cetera, and if you follow it, the information will save you months, or even years, in your writing endeavors.

Plus, it will help make your masterpiece look and feel like that of a bestselling, or famous author. At least that is my hope for you, it truly is.

Pick a Topic

Pick something that is of interest to you and/or a fictional story, if you should so wish to try that Genre of a novel.

If you cannot think of anything to write about, just remember that everyone has at least one book in them even if it is just their own personal autobiography. Those are nice to give to family, friends, acquaintances, and such. I personally recommend that each of you readers write your autobiographies, regardless of your age.

Select a topic, something that you are interested in or that you like to do. Chose something that you are knowledgeable about, or that you are good at, such as sports, interior designing, skydiving (over Lake Elsinore/Temecula, California), hot air ballooning (over Albuquerque, New Mexico), shooting pool, bowling, knitting, canoeing, butterfly watching, et cetera..., even a hobby that you want others to try.

Topics such as golf, sailing, horseback riding, or country western dancing (one of my favorites, but please do not tell anybody, alright), swimming, fishing, and the list goes on and on. Anything that you wish to convey to someone else, will work. You never know how many people (readers) will be interested in the same thing as yourself.

Examples of Topics:

I recently met a man named Bert. The topic that he picked was a very good one. He was a very smart and extremely interesting man. He had been the Skipper of John 'Duke' Wayne's *Wild Goose* ship out of Newport Beach, California for sixteen years. He wanted to write a book (true story) about his time with the Duke and his absolutely wonderful family for all of those years.

Yet, he was not an English major, he did not know how to go about writing, nor publishing his heart felt book. He was fortunate to find a journalist to help him put his memories down on paper and also a publisher who was willing to pay for the upfront fees, et cetera.

This is almost unheard of these days, however, because we are talking about the Duke, Bert was able to take advantage of that and accomplish his dream of writing part of his true-life story.

He did not have to do all of the months and years of research that I did to learn, "How to Write a Novel." My point here is, however, not that he had help with his work of art, but that he picked a great topic to write about, one that he knew well and was of interest to many readers.

The *Wild Goose* was a 136-foot former US Navy minesweeper built for World War II in Seattle, Washington. Interestingly, it was the sister ship of the well-known French explorer, *Jacques Cousteau*, 'Calypso' the ship famous in the National Geographic TV shows. These explorations were watched all around the Globe. And they were both built about the same time in a very well-known Seattle shipyard.

His book (true story) included several absolutely marvelous photos of the 'Duke', his family, and also friends like, Dean Martin, Bob Hope, Pilar (wife who was a famous Peruvian actress), Lana Turner, Barbara Read, Humphrey Bogart and wife Lauren Bacall.

 John Ford (close friend and famous director), Zane Grey (famous western novel author), Spencer Tracy, John Farrow (famous director), Maureen O'Hara, Ernest Gann (famous author of *The High and the Mighty*).

The wonderful Sammy Davis, Jr. (part of the famous Las Vegas, Nevada 'Rat Pack' which included, Francis Albert 'Frank' Sinatra, Dean 'Dino' Martin, Peter Lawford, Joey Bishop, plus a few others), as well as many other famous people of that day.

He sells it for $99 new online at Amazon, and there are some used ones for about $49. Also, this fabulous old ship, is still located in

Newport Beach today and it can be rented for parties, and/or, cruises. Bert's book is sold on the ship as well.

I used this as an example of a topic because I read and really enjoyed his book. This is just one example, however, of thousands of Topics that you may come up with from your own; real life experiences, famous or *infamous* people you have met during your lifetime.

Or, your hobbies, your travels, your interests, your education, your successes in business, acting, working, 'et cetera, et cetera, and et cetera' (remember the fabulous movie musical *The King and I*?).

I consider myself more of an infamous author as opposed to a famous one. I read somewhere on the net, that I am an *'Internationally* known mystery novelist'.

Another Example:

If I may be so bold, being the author of this little self-help book, I would like to use myself as an example as well. In the back of my little brain, for years I had an idea of writing a mystery *crime-fiction* genre, novel about a Private Investigator. I had no idea of how to write it, how to edit it, how to research it, how to publish it, nor how to market it.

As previously stated, I was not an English, nor Journalism, major. I was an International Business Administration major. I worked as a Corporate Vice President for Bank of America for twenty years in and around Los Angeles, California.

That was the topic that I finally selected to be my first novel. You may have a topic in the back of your brain as well, and now would be a terrific time to 'open your barn door' and let your idea and topic go from your 'mind to a book store' on line or near you.

I came up with my Protagonist, anti-hero, as well as to tell the truth, my alter ego, "Charles Warner Kennedy O'Brien," or just plain old 'Charlie' for short. He is a Private Detective who works out of Los Angeles, California, however, he travels all around the world, solving 'White Collar' crimes.

Like *'too big to fail'* bank embezzlements, Ponzi schemes, money laundering by major drug cartels, organized crime, as well as others with these types of illegal criminal activities.

As you can see, I picked a topic that I knew a lot about. I worked for B of A, the largest bank in the USA and the thirteenth largest in the whole world and have a great deal of knowledge of banking procedures. Also, I am a lifelong fan of Private Detectives, and Private Investigators, and have a lot of knowledge of that business as well as many others.

I could list many other great examples of some topics for your masterpiece, your first novel, however, for sake of time, just use your 'gut'. It boils down to what do you want to write about? After all, it is your book.

Next, I would like to propose to your readers some ideas, suggestions, that I feel will be very helpful in your pursuit of becoming a good, and/or better writer.

HOW TO BECOME AN <u>AUTHOR</u>:

Write like you are going to throw your manuscript away.

Write without putting any stress upon yourself. Example: "I have to finish this right away, and it has to be perfect."

Write without worrying whether your novel will turn out to be good, or not so good (bad), or whether people are going to be critical of it.

Write, have fun writing and when you get tired, or stressed out, just stop. Period. And take time to smell the roses, eat great food, drink good wine (aged or not), sweets (like me), or whatever you like to smell.

Write, give it a fair chance, just like you would any other activity that you have tried to do in your past. Read about it, do your research, and then, read some novels in the Genre that you are considering writing about. You can get great ideas on formatting your book by reading novels by well-known authors.

Your story ideas, have to come from yourself, from deep within you, not them, however, the way they 'lay out' (i.e. organize and put together), their books can help you with your design, it can assist you a lot.

If you do not find this project of writing a novel, and or book, fun or if it is stressful, upsetting, or too frustrating for you, then simply find another activity that you like to do better. There are hundreds, and hundreds, of neat things that you can do with your free time, and you will enjoy them better.

Remember, not everyone is meant to become an 'author.' Give it your best shot *first* though, before you give up on your lifelong dream. You may never have a second chance of becoming that next new bestselling writer.

Now, a *second* set of thoughts about becoming a novelist, here are some exercises. Just like any other activity (sports), exercises help you in your process to achieve your goals. These are a few, there are many others, of course.

Write a novel/book/short story of a few pages up to 10,000 words, just to warm you up and get your creative juices flowing. See how you like it, *test the waters*, so to speak. You may love it, or hate it, and this will give you a good indication of if you should pursue your writing dreams or move on to something else.

Write a novel/book/longer story of 10,000 to 100,000 words. This is the real test of your determination and desire to become a literary giant. Also, this exercise will get you to become a much better and more proficient author as well as much more skilled at writing stories. It will increase your self-confidence (self-Image as I like to call it) measurably.

Write a real, real long novel/book of 100,000 to 200,000 words. Yes, this is a lot. A real lot of words. If you can do this, and I believe that most of you readers can, writing will become second nature to you and you shall, perhaps, become a great writer, or at the very least, a much better one than you are today.

Somewhere between 10,000 and 200,000 words, you will know if you are cut out to be a literary novelist, you really will. Trust me on that. And worst-case scenario is that you say you do not like doing this, then go out and find another hobby and do it right away so that you do not waste your very valuable time.

Novel Genre:

I would like to recommend that you pick some bestselling authors in the genre in which you wish to write-in. Then after that, read some of their books to get ideas on how they structure, format, and organize their novels. Remember, you are not looking at their works to get story lines, plots, sub-plots, characters, or ideas of any kind for that matter.

The only reason that you are reading their novels, is to see their book lay-out, font style and size, length, number of words, margins, paragraphs, capitalization, format, and et cetera.

I believe if you will do this before you start your masterpiece it will help you, a great deal, when you begin to write your first novel. As an example, let's say that you want to write in the mystery, crime-fiction, thriller, or suspense Genre. Then, I would strongly suggest that you pick up, or order an eBook, by one of the following outstanding and bestselling authors:

Tom Clancy (sadly, he recently died)
Patricia Cornwall
John Grisham
Janet Evanovich
Sandra Brown
David Baldacci
Lisa Jackson

Heather Graham
Jonathan Kellerman
Faye Kellerman
These are, among many others, great mystery storytellers to choose from.

I would like to add here a few additional pointers on the subject of your topic, if I may. If your novel is a fiction book, then you must always write in the 'past tense', not the 'present tense' or the' future tense', even though that is how we generally speak. In non-fiction works, it does not matter in which tense you write, past, present or future.

In addition, please note that most publishers, or co-publishers, do not accept manuscripts (word documents/books/novels), with gratuitous sex, violence, lots of cuss words, sadistic, offensive prejudicial content, or real vulgar language. Therefore, unless you are addressing your novel to that type of market, you should obviously refrain from using that type of material for the general public.

CHAPTER TWO
MANUSCRIPTS AND CITATIONS

The most important part of writing your best-selling novel (you hope it will be anyway), is to do your 'due diligence' in researching your topic or subject matter. Unless it is a true story, of course, then you just recite it how you wish to.

In real estate they say, location, location, location is the most important thing that you can pay attention to when you are buying a piece of property. I am sure that you have heard that many, many times just as I have.

And as a writer, always remember, research, research, research, is the most important thing that you can do when you are writing your novel.

Do your research before anything else. You can do a rough outline first if you feel led to do that, as I usually do. Also, you may wish to do some additional research while you are still writing your book, for updates and such. That is a very good idea and I do that as well.

Do your journaling if it is a true story. You must have that before you can effectively start your novel, short story, or novella. Use the Library. It used to be the best way and only way to research a book.

Now days, the internet is much better, faster and easier. You can do it from your own office or home. Almost everything is on the net these days, **literally**, it is indeed. I use the internet for research all of the time. Also print-newspapers, internet news, magazines on line, friends, relatives or experts in the area that you are writing about.

Please remember, always, that if you use information, and or, research material for your novel from the internet, you must quote your source. And use the 'proper citation.' If you quote from a magazine, newspaper-print, book, novel, 'anything' at all, you must cite, and 'give credit where credit is due'.

Also, look up 'citation' on the net as well. It will be very helpful for you and it will keep you out of court and a possible law suit from the 'original writer', or source. And, you also can ask your local library, and/or another established author, about 'citations' and how to correctly use them for legal reasons.

CITATION:

Broadly speaking, a 'citation' is a reference to a published or unpublished source (i.e. not always the original source). Even more precisely, a citation is an abbreviated alphanumeric expression embedded in the body of an intellectual work that denotes an entry in the bibliographic references section of the work for the purpose of acknowledging the relevance of the works of others to the topic of discussion at the spot where the citation appears.

Generally, the combination of both the in-body citation and the bibliographic entry constitutes what is commonly thought of as a citation (whereas bibliographic entries by themselves are not).

References to single, machine-readable assertions in electronic scientific articles are known as nano-publications, a form of micro attribution.

Citation has several important purposes; to uphold intellectual honesty, to attribute prior or unoriginal work and ideas to the correct sources, to allow the reader to determine independently whether the referenced material supports the author's argument in the claimed way, and to help the reader gauge the strength and validity of the material the author has used.

The forms of citations generally subscribe to one of the generally accepted citations systems, such as the Oxford, Harvard, MLA, American Sociological Association (ASA), American Psychological Association (APA), and other citations systems, as their syntactic conventions are widely known and easily interpreted by readers.

Each of these citation systems has its own respective advantages and disadvantages relative to the trade-offs of being informative (i.e. but not too disruptive), and thus are chosen relative to the needs of the type of publication being crafted. Editors/publishers, will often specify the citation system to use.

Citation Styles:

Citation styles can be broadly divided into styles common to the Humanities and Sciences. These are identified briefly, here:

Humanities:
The Chicago Style
The Columbia Style

Evidence Explained
Harvard Referencing
MLA
The MHRA Style Guide

Law:
The Bluebook
The Legal Citation Style
British Legal Citation
Sciences, Mathematics, Engineering, Physiology, and Medicine:
The American Chemical Society Style (ACS)
American Institute of Physics (AIP)
American Mathematical Society (AMS)
Vancouver System (CSE)
Electrical and Electronics Engineers Style (IEEE)
Pechenik Citation Style
Social Sciences:
American Psychological Association (APA)
American Political Science Association (CMOS)
American Anthropological Association
American Sociological Association

CITATION MARKS:

In the case of direct citations, the boundaries of a citation are apparent from the quotation marks. The boundaries, however, of indirect citations are usually unknown. In order to clarify these subject boundaries, citation marks (,) can be used. Example:

This is sentence 1., "This is sentence 2., This is sentence 3.", (Smith et al., 2013). Here, it becomes apparent from the citation marks that the citation refers to both sentence 2 and 3, but not to sentence 1.

CITATION ISSUES:

In their research on footnotes in scholarly journals in the field of communication, Michael Bugeja and Daniela V. Dimitrova, have found that citations to Online sources have a rate of decay (as cited pages are taken down), which they call a 'half-life', that renders footnotes in those journals less useful for scholarship over time.

Other experts have found that published replications do not have as many citations as do original publications for some reason. Another important issue is citation errors, which often occur due to carelessness on either the researcher or the journal editor's part in the long publication procedure.

Experts have found that simple precautions, such as consulting the author of a cited source about proper citations, reduce the likelihood of citation errors and thus increase the quality of your research.

In addition, please check with your literary attorney, if you have one, if you have any questions about 'citations' in your novel. If you do not have one, you can find one through a friend, relative or on the internet. If you have to pay, it will be well worth every penny (dollar).

MANUSCRIPTS. FICTION:

Develop your main story line (plot) for your novel. Then develop your cast of interesting characters. They are the *real plot*, your real story. Your main character, he or she will make your book 'come alive' to the readers, your protagonist, hero or anti-hero, and in my case, my alter-ego as well.

Most novels also need a sub-plot or two, in order to make your book 'more exciting' and also keep your readers interest piqued and ready for more 'twists and turns' around every corner (page).

If your novel takes place in a foreign country, as do most of mine, include some language from that country. Have your characters speak in that language and then translate it into English so that your readers may understand and follow along. I think that it is fun to do that and many well know authors do that as well.

Use the internet, my world lingo, the library, or one of those great, "Spanish (et cetera) for Dummies" books that you can buy. I like having different languages in my novels, however, it is entirely up to you. You may not wish to do that and that is quite alright.

Again, if your novel takes place in some romantic location, exotic foreign land, or just a foreign county outside of the USA, include some history about that country incorporate it into your story/book. It will break the plot up a little bit, however, it adds to the enjoyment and interest of the reader, at least in my personal opinion. I read a bestselling authors novel last year, and it took place partly in Hong Kong.

He talked a lot about Hong Kong, now part of China, the city, and a 'fortune cookie' company. He talked a lot about the 'cookie' corporation and included several Chinese, and Mandarin, words in his book.

I found it very interesting and I learned a lot about Hong Kong, China, and Macau (Island), that I did not know. Also, if your story takes place in the good old US of A, please include some historical information about that as well. There are hundreds of great and exciting places right here at home in America.

Like all men (and some women), I love cars, all kinds of cars. A lot of readers will enjoy reading about fast cars and remember 'size' does matter when it comes to a car's HP (horse power). Some people love to say, "Go Chevy V-8, or go home."

Ever heard that old saying? I usually include some favorite vehicles in my novels with full descriptions of them and their big motors, of course.

I will have one of my book characters driving a certain car and then talk about it. If you do not like cars/trucks, or do not want to mention any in your novel, that is fine, just an idea and something that I like to do.

Please remember, you have to come up with close to 90,000 or more words, and 300 to 500 pages, for your work of art (novel). You will need, therefore, to write about something else besides your characters, and your plot, if you are going to be able to come up with that many words, trust me on that, I know.

A few vehicles that might be very impressive to write about in your novel, perhaps you could have your hero, or heroine, driving one of the following:

1960 250 GT SWB Berlinetta "Competizione." Only 74 of the roughly 170 short-wheelbase 250 cars were made in this lighter, street-legal racing version. Estimated value $8 million.

1958 Ferrari 250 GT LWB *California* Spider. This long-wheelbase convertible is one of only 50 built and features a 3.0-liter V-12 engine. Value $5 to $7 million.

1959 Porsche RSK. This small, open top silver racer is one of only 37 built and weighs just 1,200 pounds. Value $2.8 to $3.2 million.

1965 Ford GT40. A rarer series of the GT40 and considered more pure and closest to Ford's true intentions with the GT40 program. Value $2.4 to $3 million.

1968 Shelby EXP500 "*Green Hornet*" Mustang. This one of a kind car has the distinction of being used as two different prototypes. In 1968 for a never built Mustang and then later on by Shelby American, to test various new fuel injection and suspension systems. Value $2.5 to $5 million.

1955 Mercedes-Benz 300SL *Gullwing* (the all-time favorite of this author). Bought new at M-B of Hollywood by the famous actor Clark Gable, who owned the car until his death in 1960. Value $2 to $3 million.

1958 Ferrari 250GT Coupe *Speciale*. Has a one-off custom body by designer Pinin Farina. Value $1.7 to $2.1 million.

1938 Mercedes-Benz 540A. One of only 95 made that year. Original unrestored car. Value $1.5 to $1.75 million.

The Original *Batmobile*. Built in 1965 by the famous George Barris using a Lincoln Futura concept car from 1955. It was used in the 1960's ABC TV show 'Batman' staring Adam West. Value $500,000 to $2 million.

Another sub-point, or *sub-topic*, to use in your novel to increase the word count, besides the ones listed above (and there are many others by the way) are musicians and their music. Like most people I love music and good artists, I usually include some favorite singer/songwriter and mention their songs in my novels.

Everyone has their own personal favorites, and you may choose, whomever you like and wish too. Remember to use a *'citation'* when you use the lyrics of a specific artist, of course. Lots of authors do this, however, you may not wish too, and wish to include some other related information about anything that you wish to include in your book, after all, it is your novel, right?

By the way, most music fans think that the *Beatles*, or the Rolling *Stones*, are the great bands of all time. I personally, agree with them, albeit, I feel that *Fleetwood-Mac* is up there as well. Also, *Chicago*, and the *Beach Boys*.

Another example of how to increase your word count, and if you like music as much as this said author (i.e. me), does, you may, I repeat may, wish to write something about one of these One Hundred Best Guitar Players of all time (list follows here). You could pick one, or two, to write about in your novel. You can write about their personal, private, or professional lives.

Remember, should you do this, to include the proper citations for the sources where you obtain your information about them (internet, magazine, print newspaper, or online, et cetera).

In some of my own mystery novels, I have written about some all-time great musicians, such as: *Leon Patillo*, the wonderful former vocalist for Santana. He was the soloist on the million selling song *Black Magic Woman*, as well as some of the bands most popular music. Also, the Magical *Bob Dylan*, *Ringo Starr* (former Beatle) amongst several others.

One Hundred Best Guitar Players of All Time:
Jimi Hendrix Eric Clapton Jimmy Page
Keith Richards Jeff Beck B. B. King
Chuck Berry Eddie Van Halen Duane Allman
Pete Townshend George Harrison Stevie Ray Vaughan
Albert King David Gilmour Freddy King
Derek Trucks Neil Young Les Paul
James Burton Carlos Santana Chet Atkins
Frank Zappa Buddy Guy Angus Young
Tony Iommi Brian May Bo Diddley
Johnny Ramone Scotty Moore Elmore James
Ry Codder Billy Gibbons Prince
Curtis Mayfield John Lee Hooker Randy Rhoads
Mick Taylor The Edge Steve Cropper
Tom Morello Mick Ronson Mike Bloomfield

PROFESSOR ALAN DALE DICKINSON

Hubert Sumlin Mark Knopfler Link Wray
Jerry Garcia Stephen Stills Jonny Greenwood
Muddy Waters Ritchie Blackmore Johnny Marr
Clarence White Otis Rush Joe Walsh
John Lennon Albert Collins Rory Gallagher
Peter Green Robbie Robertson Ron Asheton
Dickey Betts Robert Fripp Johnny Winter
Duane Eddy Slash (Guns n' Roses) Leslie West
T-Bone Walker John McLaughlin Richard Thompson
Jack White Robert Johnson John Frusciante
Kurt Cobain Dick Dale Joni Mitchell
John Fahey Mike Campbell Buddy Holly
Robbie Krieger Willie Nelson Lou Reed
Nels Cline Eddie Hazel Joe Perry
Andy Summers J. Mascis James Hetfield
Carl Perkins Dave Davies Dimebag Darrell
Paul Simon Bonnie Raitt Tom Verlaine
Peter Buck Roger McGuinn Bruce Springsteen
Steve Jones Alex Lifeson Thurston Moore
Lindsey Buckingham

Note: *In my opinion, anyway, music is definitely wonderful food for the Soul, and your mind, as well as one of the greatest joys of life.*

If your fiction novel is a murder mystery about detectives, private investigators, gangsters, or the like, you may wish to discuss what sort of guns or weapons your hero, and characters, carry. I write about a PI (private investigator).

I talk about what sort of guns he uses, I describe them, make, models, kind of bullets that they use, et cetera. Just another suggestion.

Men read more detective, crime-fiction Genre novels than women do. And they usually know a lot about guns, and weapons of all sorts, and like to read about them. Some women also like guns and know how to use them and also know more about them than I do.

Romance novels. Women love romantic books just as much as men love Sci Fi, futuristic, western, and mystery novels. I heard that 'Ms. Danielle Steel', the very well-known romance author, is one of the wealthiest women in America.

Please do not quote (cite me) on that as I am not for sure. It is a well-known fact that romance novels, and novellas, bring in big bucks for those authors.

If I may be candid, once again, with you readers of my little self-help book on "How to Write a Novel", I like to read a good romance novel every once and a while.

Anyway, it is alright for a real man to read romance novels, as well as to cry if he feels like he needs too. In my opinion, anyway.

MANUSCRIPTS. NON-FICTION:

If your novel, or book, is a true story and not a work of fiction, you still have lots of ways to increase the length of your book. You can develop your main character (i.e. you, or your relatives, friends, or whomever you include in your book), in much more detail than you usually would in a short true story.

You may wish to include historical background on yourself, or them, genealogy as it were, in length. Also, as mentioned previously, you can include lots of information, and details, of the location, and or locations, where your true story (or autobiography), took place.

CHAPTER THREE
SELECT YOUR FORMAT

FORMAT:

Remember the format of your novel reflects who you are as an *individual*. You can use fancy keystrokes, capitalize some words, italicize other words (personally I like to do that), and make some words bold. There are lots, and lots, of fun, artistic and creative things that you can do with your novel besides just plain, *ordinary* Times New Roman font. There are many ways to personalize your masterpiece. Yes, there truly are, indeed.

FONT STYLE:

Some examples:

Calibri, Arial, Book Antiqua, Cambria, Constantia, Century Gothic, Engravers MT, Franklin Gothic Heavy, Lucida, Sams, Microsoft Sans Serif, Mongolian Baiti, Papyrus, Rockwell Extra Bold, Sim Sun, Verdana, Wingdings, and many, many more to choose from.

I recommend that you start out with Times New Roman, and then later on, when you have more experience, you may wish to try one of these other fonts. I believe that this said author (i.e. me), used 'Calibri' font for this little book. I do, however, use Times New Roman for all of my mystery novels.

Times New Roman Font (type), is the norm for most publishers and published works, although it does vary, so be yourself and enjoy going 'outside of the box' with your, own individual style.

Women authors seem to be more adept and artistic in this area than do the male authors for some reason. FYI, some of my favorite mystery authors are women, one example, Ms. *Nora Roberts*, she rocks.

FONT SIZE:

Some examples:

10 point, 12 point, 14 point, 16 point, and so forth.

For most published works, normal size is 12 point, however, once again you can 'change that up' if you wish too. Remember it is your novel/book after all, right. I like 12 point, however, I also use 14 point, as my eyesight is not what it used to be.

NUMBERS:

When you use numbers in your novel, or book, or novella, or autobiography remember that normally you should write them out in letters. Example:

Write *ten* instead of 10, and *two* instead of 2, and *three* instead of 3, and so on and so forth. There are exceptions to this, just like there are exceptions to most of the other rules 'suggested' in this author's self-help book.

Note before you use the numbers 'in lieu' of the letters for your numbers in your novel, you should check with an English expert or, another author, just to be safe.

PARAGRAPHS:

The first paragraph in each new chapter should not be indented, it should be all the way to the left gutter margin. The rest of the paragraphs in the chapter then should be indented about five to ten spaces. Yes, this will vary a lot between authors, remember, they are very creative and you can be as well. Pick your *own* style.

The first paragraph in each new chapter should have several words capitalized. All authors are different, I like to capitalize the first five words. You may wish to cap three, or ten, I recently noted a good author capped the whole first line of his first sentence, another capped only one word. To each his/her own.

CHAPTER HEADINGS:

Chapter headings should be larger than the Font you are using for the regular text. Say you are using 12 point for your novel, then use 16 point or 18 point size for your chapter headings. Also, the headings should be centered and at the top of each new chapter.

They need to be on a new, fresh, page and not on the same page with another chapter. They can be way at the top of the new page, or they can be spaced down somewhat. I like to space down about 3" myself, however, feel free to suit yourself, there is no hard and fast rule for this point either.

In the paragraph which is in the *middle* of your chapter, you may also wish to capitalize a few words. I like to cap three words. You can do one, three, the whole line, or none. It is up to you. The length of your paragraph should be five to ten lines, with no more than about twelve lines per paragraph.

If you wish to write only three lines in each paragraph, or 20 lines, that will be quite alright as well. If you read some bestselling authors in the Genre that you are attempting to write in, you will see this point varies greatly.

If you wish, like I do, you may *Italicize*, or **bold** face, some words in each chapter of your novel. I feel that this technique improves the look and feel of your novel. You cannot underline as the printers are not able to reproduce these for some unknown reason. Remember, if you do not want to use these little tools, you do not have too.

You are required to put a page number at the bottom of each and every page. Also you must put the name of your novel and your name at the top of each page. You must *alternate* these so that on one page, say on the left side of your book, you have your name, then on the right side, you can have the novels name.

If you do not follow me, just glance at a bestselling book and you will see what I mean. This is very difficult to do with software unless you are a computer guru. If you have trouble, just ask a relative or friend who has done this type of work before.

Remember to double space your manuscript while working on it (it is much easier to edit and/or make changes if your novel is double spaced), and then remember to single space it before you submit it to your publisher or you self-publish it. Print your draft on white paper and be sure to only use one side of the paper.

Some new writers use both sides to save money and or the trees, however, it is way too hard to read and, or edit if there is printing on both sides of the paper.

Also, use plain white paper. Men always do this, however, since women are more artistic, sometimes they use colored paper. They may even use colored type/print, like they do in emails, however, this should be avoided unless you really know what you are doing and are an experienced author.

HEADINGS:

You are required to put a heading (i.e. header), at the top of each and every page of your novel. On one side you must put your name as the author, and on the other side, the title of your book. It is also necessary that you alternate your page headings so that half of the novel will have your name at the very top, and the other half of your book, will have the title of your work at the top.

This is a simple form of advertising you and your novel both, however, I am guessing, I am not quite sure why writers/publishers do this, are you?

Also, you should use larger font (type) for your headings than the font that you use in the text of your work, so that your name and book title will be noticed better by the reader.

This activity can be difficult, at least it was for myself, unless you are a software guru, of course, and as you should have discerned by now, I am clearly not one.

FOOTINGS:

In addition, you are required to put page number footings (i.e. footers), on every page. You should put the number and not the letters ('1' and not one), of course. Also, you should not put Page 1, just put the 1. Doing this is also very tricky and you may have to get someone to assist you with this process, as with the headings, just as I did. If I may be very candid with you.

GRAMMAR:

Checking your grammar is another very crucial part of your novel writing process. For those of you who were an English, or Journalism major at University, this is not that difficult at all. For those of us who were International Business Administration majors, or some other major, however, this is very, very difficult as well as very time consuming. Indeed.

The aforementioned grammar information is presented in brief, as this is meant just to be an overview and not an English grammar book. You could, and should, probably buy and read one of those good English composition, grammar and spelling books online, or at your book store. Do this before you start your bestselling novel, if you have the time.

Building Sentences:

A proper sentence has subjects and predicates. A subject is a noun, pronoun, or phrase. A predicate tells about the subject.

Four kinds of sentences and what they do: Declarative sentences (statements), Interrogative sentences (questions), Imperative sentences (requests), and Exclamatory sentences (exclamations).

Three ways to build a sentence: Use a simple sentence (she eats), a compound sentence (she asked me to the dance, and I said yes), or a complex sentence (The mechanical dinosaur in the museum had a short circuit, it started to dance).

When words are not a sentence: This is called a Fragment. Example: "Slipping down the muddy bank and plopping into the river." Also, a run-on sentence does not have proper punctuation. Example: "It may rain take your umbrella."

Nouns and verbs work together: Examples: "I am the cheese." "You are going to get into trouble for this."

Parts of Speech:

Nouns. Are persons, places, animals, things, or ideas.

Pronouns. Are words that take the place of proper nouns.

Verbs. Are words that show action or being. Whatever you are doing can be expressed by a proper verb.

Adjectives. Are words that tell us more about a noun, or a pronoun. It also describes, or modifies, a noun.

Adverbs. Are words that tell us more about a verb, an adjective, or another adverb.

Prepositions. Are words that show the relationship of one word in a sentence to another word. They tell us where something is, or where it is going, or when something happens, or the relationship between a noun or pronoun and another word in a sentence.

Conjunctions. Are words that join other words or parts of sentences together. Example: David *and* Desiree' are husband *and* wife.

Interjections. Are special words that show strong feelings or emotions like excitement, happiness, horror, shock, sadness, pain, anger and/or disgust.

Style and Usage:

Punctuation. Use apostrophes when abbreviating (i.e. "I'm sorry that she's coming after you've left."). Also use Colons, Commas, Dashes, Ellipses (i.e. ...), Exclamation Points, Hyphens, Parentheses, Periods, Quotation Marks, Semicolons, and Underlining where appropriate. Exception, for your novel you should use Italics instead of underlining.

Capitalization. You should always capitalize; the first word in each sentence, the pronoun 'I', proper nouns, proper adjectives, and titles that show rank or position of people when used with their names. Examples: Captain, Chief, Dr., King, Mr., Ms., or President.

Spelling. Spelling words in the Kings English, or any language, can be very tricky. When you are in doubt, it is always a good idea to use spell check, if you have it, or good old Mr. Webster's dictionary, if you do not have spell check on your computer. Nine rules that will assist you greatly as they did me.

1) when you add Full to any word, drop the second L,

2) When you add a Y or a suffix that begins with a vowel (a, e, I, o, u) to a word that ends with a silent E, drop the silent E.

3) When adding, the suffix ING to a word that ends with IE drop the E and change the I to Y,

4) When adding a suffix that begins with a consonant (all letters that aren't vowels, or Y), do not drop the silent E.,

5) Double the final consonant when you are adding a suffix that begins with a vowel (Ing, ed) to a word that ends with a vowel and a consonant (hop, refer).

6) to make most nouns plural, you just add S, however, there are some exceptions,

7) Drop the Y and add IES if the letter in front of the final Y is a consonant,

8) Add S to most nouns that end in O to make them plural, and,

9) Using I and E. Always place I before E, except after C, or when sounding like A as in neighbor and weigh.

Double negatives. Negative means no. A negative word expresses a meaning that is the opposite of positive. It says that something is not, rather than that something is.

Homonyms. Or, homophones, are words that are spelled differently, have different meanings, but are pronounced alike. Examples: Allowed/aloud, ant/aunt, ate/eight, bear/bare, blue/blew, break/brake, bury/berry, capital/capitol, and dear/deer.

Confused and misused words. Some examples here: accent/ascent, accept/except, adapt/adept, coma/comma, lose/loose, umpire/empire.

Shrinking words. A contraction is one word that was once two words. When you make a contraction, your simple squeeze together (or contract) two words into one word. Examples: I am/I'm, I would/I'd, I will/I'll, I have/I've, who is'/who's, are not/aren't, what is/what's.

Compound words. A compound word is made up of two or more words. Sometimes one word isn't enough to express an idea, name an object, or say what a writer is trying to express, so people make up compound nouns and adjectives. They come in three ways, Closed, Open, and Hyphenated.

Initials, acronyms, and abbreviations. Initials are just a kind of abbreviation. Sometimes expressions or the names of things are known by their initials, (i.e. their first letters). Examples: A.D.D. =

Alan Dale Dickinson (this said author), AD = Anno Domini, B.C. = British Columbia, CD-ROM = Compact Disk-Read Only Memory.

An acronym is a kind of abbreviation as well. It is a word made out of the first letters of other words. Some Examples: NOW = National Organization for Women, RADAR = Radio Detecting and Ranging, WHO = World Health Organization.

Abbreviations help to speed up your writing, you may sometimes use a shortened form of a word, and or, phrase.

(Citation: Scholastic Guides Inc. Marvin Terban. New York, New York 1993).

FINAL REMINDER:

As this said author previously mentioned, please watch out for those dreaded **correctos** (i.e. those words that are spelled correctly, albeit, used incorrectly in a sentence). They are your real enemy, not regular ordinary typos (spelling errors), words spelled incorrectly. Thank God for spell check, right? I would be absolutely lost and 'up the creek without a paddle' without spell check.

And yes, those pesky little *correctos* are your (and my) worst nightmare!

CHAPTER FOUR
MARGINS AND COPYRIGHTS

PRINT Margins are normally 1" all the way around your novel. On the right, left, top and bottom, although that can vary. Your novel margins may be 1/4" to 3/4" on the top, right and bottom, under some circumstances, however, it must be at least 1" on the left side due to the bookbinding. I like to use around 1 " myself.

As I stated before, a friendly reminder here, double space while writing your rough draft document (novel). Also, remember to always do a rough draft, or two, before you publish your new book. It is much easier to edit the book that way than if it is single spaced.

Of course, you need to remember to single space when you are finished with your editing. All novels should be single spaced once they are completed and prudently edited.

Note: This self-help book on *How to Write a Novel* is an exception to that rule as it is *double* spaced, instead of single spaced. The reason for this is in order to make it easier, faster, and more understandable for new authors. I hope that you will understand, and I also hope that it will accomplish my goal.

And, always remember to *justify* the right margin in your novel. Your computer software will automatically block your left margin for you, however, for some reason you will usually have to make the right margin blocked and straight. It looks much better that way, although I have seen some books without it.

I do strongly suggest that your novel's right margin be blocked/straight, just like your left margin. It will look better and more professional that way. Some people refer to this as 'justifying' your right margin.

Just to mention a few important organizational points that I do not believe that I talked about before, they are listed here:

Do not leave any white (blank) space at the top of each page, except at the top of each new chapter page, where it is alright to have white spacing. You should indent every paragraph *except* the very first sentence at the start of each chapter.

And, number chapter headings with letters, not numbers (use one and not 1). Also, do not put the word 'Chapter' in front of your chapter ((do not type Chapter one, just type One).

And, you should make your one (and all your chapter headings), larger than the font (type) size, of the rest of your text (material) for that following chapter.

Then remember to always capitalize the first letter of your chapter headings (One and not one). Now, change EM dashes to dash, dash (i.e. - -) and use three dots with no spaces for your ellipse (...). Use scene break, if you are writing a novel, instead of blank scenes (i.e. - * -).

Also, use headers (i.e. your name and the title of your novel) on the top of each and every page, and they must alternate, of course.

And, put the page number at the very bottom, footer, of each page. This is very important for obvious reasons. Use *Italics* instead of underlining, underscoring your selected words. For some unknown reason, publishers cannot print books with underlining in them.

And also, put double quotes around dialogue between characters in your novel rather than single quotes ("quote" and not 'quote').

COPYRIGHT:

It is crucial, and let me repeat myself, it is vital that you file your Copyright (legal ownership), to your work, before you publish, or show it to any perspective publishers. This must be done with the Library of Congress. They are located at:

Library of Congress
Copyright Office - TX
101 Independence Avenue, SE
Washington, DC 20559 - 6222

The rights to your *Masterpiece* (new novel), are not legally *protected* until they have been filed, and you have completed the whole Copyright process, with this said office. Please I beseech you to take this point extremely seriously. You may call them, or email them, if you have any questions.

And as a first-time writer, you will have some questions, I know that I had several. They are usually helpful if you tell them that you are a first- time author and that this is your first Copyright. They are very helpful, albeit, extremely busy. They process millions of copyrights a year.

I have been to D.C. before, fabulous place to visit, 'back in the day' and now I plan on one day going to D.C. again and visiting the Copyright office. It would be extremely interesting; do you not agree?

You can do the copyright process on line, and then send to them a hard (paper) copy of your manuscript for their files, this is a requirement. Also, you must send a copy of your work within thirty days of your computer filing.

This may be the **most** important thing for you to do in your long list of the very necessary steps to produce your bestseller. Once again, obtaining the copyright to your novel is vital. It is indeed. If you do not protect your project (book) and someone else uses your personal, and hard work, you will have no recourse against them, whatsoever. Period. This said copyright will protect your ownership throughout the USA. It may not, however, protect your book rights in foreign countries.

You need to check with a copyright attorney to be sure. Also, you should look up 'copyrights' on the internet, and call their office in Washington, DC, as well as check with a good attorney who is very familiar with copyrights. Please note that I am not an attorney, and also, I am not that familiar with copyright laws.

Here I am just trying to assist you, a little bit, with your copyrighting process. And also, to point out to you how extremely crucial that it is to the legal ownership of your novel.

Copyright Term:

I believe, albeit I am not sure, that your copyright, once you have properly filed it in DC, will last, a) for your lifetime, and b) for an additional 70 years after your death. *Please* check on this for your own protection, alright?

What is a Copyright?

Let us review a few things about copyrights, if I may. Copyright is a form of protection provided by the laws of the United States of America, to the *authors* of "original works of authorship," including literary, dramatic, musical, artistic, and certain other intangible works of art. This said protection is available for both published and unpublished works.

Exclusive Rights of Copyright Laws:

The initial owner of the copyright generally has the exclusive right to do all of the following:

To reproduce the work in copies or photo records.

To prepare derivative works based upon that said work.

To distribute copies or photo records of the work to the public by sale or other transfer of ownership, or by rental, lease, and/or lending.

And, also in the case of literary, musical, dramatic, and choreographic works, pantomimes, and pictorial, graphic, or sculptural works, including the individual images of a motion picture or other audiovisual work, and to display the work publicly.

And, in the case of sound recordings, to perform the work publicly by means of certain digital audio transmissions.

Owner of Copyright:

Only those deriving their rights through the author can own copyright in the said work. The author may transfer all, and or part, of the copyright to someone else, should they wish too. Copyright protection exists from the time the work is created and fixed in some tangible form. The copyright immediately becomes the property of the author upon that fixation.

In the case of a work having more than one author, the authors are co-owners of the said copyright, unless there is an agreement to the contrary. In the case of a work made for hire, the employer, not the employee, is presumed to be the author.

A copyright may also be conveyed by operation of Law and may be bequeathed by a Will or pass at the death of the copyright owner as personal property by the applicable Laws of intestate succession.

Divisibility of Copyright:

Any, or all of the exclusive rights of the copyright owner, or any subdivision of those rights, may be transferred separately. The transfer, however, of any exclusive right is not valid unless the transfer is in writing and signed by the owner of the rights conveyed (or the owner's duly authorized agent).

The transfer of a nonexclusive right does not require a written document, but a written document may afford priority to the licensee in certain situations. Therefore, it is recommended.

Advantages of Copyright Recordation:

While the recordation of a transfer or document pertaining to a copyright is not mandatory, there are several advantages to said recordation. These include:

Under certain conditions, recordation establishes priorities between conflicting transfers, or between a conflicting transfer and nonexclusive license.

Recordation establishes a public record of the contents of the transfer or document.

Recordation of a document in the Copyright Office, in Washington, DC, provides the advantage of "constructive notice," a legal concept meaning that members of the pubic are deemed to have knowledge of the facts stated in the document and cannot claim otherwise.

Section 205 of the Copyright Act says that recordation of a document in the Copyright Office gives all person's constructive notice of the facts stated in the recorded document, but only if:

a) The document or material attached to it specifically indentifies the work to which it pertains so that, after the document is indexed by the Register of Copyrights, it would be revealed by a reasonable search under the works Title (or registration number), of that said work;

And,

b) Registration has been made for the work.

Recordation may be required to perfect a security interest, according to Case Law.

Recordation of Transfers and Other Documents:

Whether or not a copyrighted work has been registered with the U.S. Copyright Office, owners of these works often enter into agreements that affect their ownership rights.

They may authorize others to use their works, even giving someone else control over ways in which a work is used. Documents pertaining to agreements regarding copyrights may be recorded in the Copyright Office.

Recording a document is voluntary in most cases. However, the Law encourages documents recordation by conferring certain legal advantages, including priority between conflicting transfers and 'constructive notice', if certain requirements are met.

Any document pertaining to a copyright may be recorded as long as the person submitting it complies with the procedures set forth in the U.S. Copyright publications. These requirements for certain other types of documents are not covered herein.

Those documents include notices of Termination, Visual Arts registry, Shareware registry, online service provider designation of agent, identification of Anonymous or Pseudonymous authors, author death statements, and a few others.

Note: You should contact your copyright attorney, or the U.S. Copyright Office with any questions concerning any Copyright questions, any at all.

CHAPTER FIVE
LENGTH AND PRICING

Length:

What length do you wish your novel, novella, autobiography or short story to be? Long, short or in between? It is entirely up to you if you are self-publishing. If you have a publisher, they will tell you how long to make it.

Normally, most bestselling authors write 70,000 to 90,000 words, with 300 to 500 pages for fictional works, although that varies a lot depending upon the author, publisher, or if it is a non-fiction work. Non-fiction books would normally run much fewer words and be shorter in length.

I am using numbers *here* 'in lieu' of letters, for sake of time. And, also to make it easier for you to understand what I am trying to communicate to you, remember, though that you should always use letters and not numbers in your novel.

FYI: I have included here a more detailed required word count listing for those readers whom are detailed oriented, like myself.

Romance Novels:
Contemporary Romance-Short 50,000 to 75,000
Contemporary Romance-Long 75,000 to 120,000
Historical Romance-Short 50,000 to 85,000
Historical Romance-Long 85,000 to 120,000

Fantasy Romance 50,000 to 120,000
Paranormal Romance 50,000 to 120,000
Sci-Fi Romance 50,000 to 120,000
Romantic Suspense 75,000 to 120,000
Mystery Romance 60,000 to 120,000
Gothic Romance 65,000 to 75,000

General Fiction:
Included-length for all 60,000 to 120,000
Of the *following*:
Mainstream
Historical
Action
Suspense
Thriller
Espionage Light Horror
Science Fiction
Fantasy
Paranormal
Mystery
Crime
Cozy Mystery

Young *Adult*:
Ages 12 - 17 40,000 to 50,000

In addition, most publishers are not interested in seeing manuscripts (novels) with less than a 50,000-word count for any Genre other than young adult books.

Also, for young adult books, the following may be of assistance to you: The protagonist in your story should be an adolescent. The story should be a coming-of-age story for young people.

The subject matter and storyline will be appropriate to the age and experience of the main character.

The story must contain the basic elements of fiction (i.e. character, plot, setting, theme, and style). The plot can contain several major characters, but one character should emerge as the focus of the story.

Themes will be relevant and appropriate to the problems and struggles of teenagers within their own time period, regardless of the Genre. Language, complexity and conflict resolution must be age appropriate.

Know your audience and do not insult your reader's intelligence. The main characters will be young adults between the ages of 12 and 17.

The story must be engaging and involve issues the young adult readers can relate to. The main character should be leading a normal teenage lifestyle but should have to face a serious *crisis* during your story.

Avoid being preachy and overly predictable. The main characters should be fundamentally good *human* beings. They may be unhappy or in difficult circumstances, but at heart they should be good teenagers, side characters may or may not be so nice. There should be adult role models in your story, a character the hero or heroine can turn to if they choose to.

And, profanity in the dialogue is permitted (that is how some young adults talk after all) but should not be excessive and should be appropriate to that situation. No casual use of profanity should be used by the hero or heroine in their everyday conversations.

Smoking, drug use or alcohol abuse by the main character is discouraged, unless used to show character growth. Even though you see lots of these types of actions by the main characters on TV shows and at the movies. Drug or alcohol use by secondary characters is acceptable, but it should also show character development.

Descriptions of violence should be kept to a minimum. And, no excessive on-stage violence will be accepted, Period. (sexual harassment, mistreatment of children, abuse of any kind, nor cruelty to animals, et cetera).

Examples of themes that may be explored in young adult novels: peer pressure to have sex, to drink, to use drugs, or to join a gang; honesty and lawfulness; insider versus outsider; materialism and teenage social pressure.

Also, usually they use 30 chapters with about 10 pages in each chapter. About 300 words per page and about 3000 words per chapter, remember, approximately, or, 15 chapters with 20 pages each.

You choose for yourself, what you think looks like your style, your *sassy*. Once again, this also can vary, a lot. If you are a self-publisher or a co-publisher, it is your decision, entirely.

You, as my honest reader, may say to yourself, right about now, "I can never write that many words." Well of course you cannot at one sitting. You should allow yourself, 2 to 6 hours a day, five days a week to work on your novel.

Take Saturday and Sunday off, play golf, do Yoga, dance, go to the beach, go to the mountains, hike, go to Church, swim, do something that lets your little mind rest for two days.

You sit when you write therefore you need to get out of the office/house and get some needed exercise. It will help you keep fresh. Also, it is quite alright to take 6 to 12 months, or even longer, to finish your Masterpiece.

I try, emphasize the word try, to write a new Work about every 6 months. How long you take, does not matter, it truly does not. The important thing to remember at this important point in time, is that this, is:

Your Work of Art, your Alpha and your Omega, your Beginning and your End Result, your Life Dream, your life goal, your masterpiece, and hopefully, your bestselling novel.

Therefore, give it your best effort, give it your all, you never know what you can achieve once you set your mind to it. After all, I even amazed myself, with what a non-English major, retired bank Corporate Vice President, who is not a great speller nor grammatical accomplished author, during the past three years (twenty-seven novels and books).

If not a great 'Internationally known mystery novelist', which by the way I am perhaps not, I am most certainly, a very *prolific* one.

This may be the only book that you ever write, so enjoy it and make it the 'best it can be.' And if it turns out to be just one of many novels that you write, you still should enjoy writing it and have fun. Otherwise, it may be time to find another vocation, hobby and, or passion, right?

Pricing:

I could write a whole chapter on the subject of pricing your novel. I hold a Bachelors of Arts Degree in Business Administration, including marketing, from the very well -respected California State University. To save time and money (and as we used to say at Bank of America, "Time is Money". (I was a Corporate Vice President and Business Banking Officer, in the World Corporate Lending Group, at Band of America for twenty years, in and around Los Angeles, California).

Paperbacks:

This was the most prevalent form of producing a novel, book, in previous days. It is still widely used today and it is an easy, and fast way to get your novel 'out there'.

You may wish to set your price, being a new novelist, at about:

$5.99 to $29.99 dollars (US dollars). The international prices are different due to the foreign currency rates. You will have to research that with your co-publisher.

The minimum is 'normally' from $5.99 to a maximum of $99.99 (USD).

Very few new authors sell paperback novels for more than $6.00 to $30.00. Also, very few bestselling authors price their paperbacks for more than $30.00 to $100.00. I would have to guess from $7.99 to $9.99.

Hardbacks/Hard Covers:

A minimum of around $29.99 up to a maximum of $2,999.00, would be considered normal, I believe anyway. And if the book has a lot of nice Art Work, and or photos, they may price their novel at thousands of dollars.

EBooks:

You may wish to set your price, being a new author, at about:

$.99 to $9.99 (USD). Once again, the international prices will vary considerably.

The minimum is 'normally' from $ .99 to $199.00

Once again, as a new and unproven writer, you cannot ask for a high price for your paperback, hardbound, or eBook. If you do, they just simply will not sell. Period. I would suggest that you start out at $.99 (i.e. I use $.99 usually), to $2.99, and then later on adjust the price to the going rate after you sell some units.

This form (eBooks) is the most popular method of publishing in the world today. And, it would appear that it will continue to increase each year as the paperbacks, and hardcover books, decrease.

National Fiction Book Award Winners:

I believe that it may be of interest to your fiction authors, at this time, to list some outstanding writers of that genre. It may be time well spent for you to read some of these well-known and successful authors to see just how they put together and organize their novels. Remember, do not read to get story line ideas, you must have those in your brain. Read them to see what kind of format, outlines et cetera.

Prior year's winners were Louise Erdrich's "The Round House" and Jesmyn Ward "Salvage the Bones". This year's winners were Thomas Pynchon "Bleeding Edge", George Saunders, and Jhumpa Lahiri "The Lowland." Also, Elizabeth Graver "The End of the Point", Joan Silber "Fools", and, Tom Drury "Pacific."

And, Kate DiCamillo and Cynthia Kadohata won for young people's literature. E. L. Doctorow and Maya Angelou. Frank Bidart and Andrei Codrescu for poetry as well as Lawrence Wright and George Packer for non-fiction.

Some not awarded, yet honorably mentioned, were, Johathan Lethem "Dissident Gardens", Donna Tartt "The Goldfinch", and Claire Messud "The Woman Upstairs".

Marketing:

The marketing of your new book/novel/ or short story is another difficult and very long process, very long, and it shall be discussed in a future self-help book on that topic by this said author.

Along with some more insight into the pricing feature of your literary work of art, amongst some other information that was not shared in this short self-help book for the sake of time and space.

CHAPTER SIX
EDITING IS YOUR KEY

You will need a good editor for your literary work of art. I repeat myself, I hope that is alright with your readers (and I do that a lot in my novels for some unknown reason), a *good* one. Even if you are a great speller, and use good grammar, it is very difficult to find your *own* errors. Trust me on that. I am not a perfect speller, thank God for Spell Check.

Also, my grammar leaves a lot to be desired. Luckily for me, I am a great storyteller of crime-fiction mystery novels. At least according to my old publisher who was a very knowledgeable suspense/detective writer herself, as well as a publisher of many mystery novels. My point being, that if I can write a novel, anyone can, literally.

I have written twenty-seven (27) novels, novellas, short stories, self-help books, et cetera. Some of them are the same books, translated into different foreign languages. I knew nothing of the information that I have presented to you herein when I started out on my writing adventure three years ago.

There are about another 101 additional things that would be helpful to you in your pursuit of literary fame, however, if you use just the ones that I have included in this short self-help book, *How to Write a Novel*, you can write a good novel or book, and people will read it.

Keep in mind that there is a book **critic** born every minute. So please do not let unnecessary criticism unset you and certainly do not let it stop your creative juices from continuing on in your pursuit of happiness and writing.

I have had some, albeit, not many, literary critics. I just tell them that I agree with them. My novels/books/short stories are not that great, albeit, they are very entertaining mysteries, or so I have been told anyway.

Then I add that I have novels being sold in ten foreign countries: Canada, Mexico, The UK (England), Germany, France, Italy, Spain, Brazil, India and Japan.

And then, I ask them how many novels that they have written? Also, I ask how many countries their books are being sold in. Then usually, after a long pause, they become very quiet and a lot less critical. Interesting, do you not think?

I have sold an eBook novel in the UK written in Russian. Several in the UK in English. Two in France, one in Spain as well as many in the USA, of course.

Good editors are expensive unfortunately, however, you can usually find a friend or relative who was an English or Journalism major at the University. If you can afford to pay a professional editor, that is preferable, naturally.

Some co-publishers like Amazon (KDP), offer very reasonable editing fees, as well as great assistance with covers and designing of your literary work.

Things to really watch out for are what I call "words spelled correctly (therefore they do *not* show up on your spell check) that are used incorrectly". I made up a unique name for them, *correctos*. They are not typos. A few examples are:

form/from
due/do
hay/hey
their/there
went/tent
bent/sent
sun/son
me/we
worry/hurry
steal/steel
off/of
seat/eat
see/sea
list/missed
sing/wing
to/too
who/grew
live/give
than/that
king/bring
you/your
also/always
lie/tie
it/is
see/me

and/man
call/all
begin/within
say/way
made/maid
steak/stake

I am sure that you can think of many more examples similar to these few that I have pointed out here.

Other things to especially 'watch out' for when writing, are what I call "missing words" (i.e. words that are accidently left out of your text (story), that complete your sentence (thought). Spell check will not catch these type of errors, obviously, and only a good editor will find them for you.

A few examples are:

"...you never what..." instead of "...you never *know* what..."

"...and wife..." instead of "...and *his* wife..."

No question mark after you ask a question... (no?)

B. of A. instead of Bank of America

"...ask for a high for your book..." instead of "...ask for a high *price* for your book..."

"...important thing you are writing..." instead "...important thing *when* you are writing..."

One more thing to add here, if I may, words used at the *start* of each sentence that are accidently not capitalized. Examples:

PROFESSOR ALAN DALE DICKINSON

Small I instead of capital I

also, instead of Also

apple instead of Apple

open instead of Open

et cetera

Here, at this point in my little book, I would like to present to you readers, if I may, a few examples from someone who possesses absolutely outstanding writing skills, as well as her very interesting thoughts concerning author's that she included in one of her wonderful mystery novels.

I just *love* the 'stuff' she writes, as well as the style that she writes it in, I truly do. And I hope that you will feel the same way as I do.

Ms. *Nora Roberts* (a.k.a. J. D. Robb), is a Rock Star of writers, she is indeed.

Please note the quotes here as they are her perfect words not my own:

"...If writers were often considered odd, writers' conferences, were oddities in themselves. They certainly could not be considered quiet or organized or stuffy. Like nearly every other of the two hundred or so participants, she stood in one of the dozen lines at 8:00 am for registration.

From the laughing and calling and embracing, it was obvious that many of the writers and would-be authors knew one another. There was an air of congeniality, shared knowledge and camaraderie. Overlaying it all was excitement."

"Still, more than one member stood in the noisy lobby like a child lost in a shipwreck, clinging to a folder or briefcase as though it were a life preserver and staring about with awe or simple confusion.

Lee could appreciate the feeling, though she looked calm and very poised as she accepted her packet and pinned her badge to the mint-green lapel of her lovely blazer.

Concentrating on the business at hand, she found a chair in a corner and skimmed the schedule for Hunter's workshop. With a dawning smile, she took out a pen and underlined it."

"Creating Horror through Proper Atmosphere and Emotion."

"Bingo, she thought, capping her pen. She'd make certain she had a front-row seat. A glance at her watch showed her that she had three hours before Hunter began to speak. Never one to take chances, she took out her notebook to skim over the questions she'd listed, while people filed by her or merely loitered, chatting."

"If I get rejected again, I'm going to put my head in the oven." Your oven is electric, Judy." "It's the thought that counts." Amused Lee began to listen to the passing comments with half an ear while she added a few more questions. "And, when they brought in my breakfast this morning, there was a 500-page manuscript under my plate.

Then I completely lost my appetite." "That's nothing. I got one in my office last week written in calligraphy, 150,000 words of flowing script." Editors, Lee mused. Lee could tell them a few stories about some of the submissions that found their way to Celebrity (her magazine)."

"...He said his editor hacked his first chapter into pieces so he's going into mourning before the rewrites." "I always go into mourning before rewrites. It's after a rejection that I seriously consider taking up basket weaving as a profession." "Did you hear Jeffries is here again trying to peddle that awful manuscript about the woman with acrophobia and telekinesis?

I can't believe he won't let that novel die a quiet death. When's your next murder mystery coming out?" "In August. It's poison" "Darling, that's no way to talk about your work."

"As they passed by her, Lee caught the variety of tones, some muted, some sophisticated, and some followed the same wide range. Amazed, she watched one-man swoop by in a long, dramatic black cape.

Definitely an odd group, Lee thought, but she warmed to them. It was true she confined her skill to articles and profiles, but at heart she was a storyteller. Her position on the magazine had been hard-earned, and she'd built her world around it."

"For all her ambition, Lee had a firm fear of rejection that kept her own manuscript unfinished, buried in a drawer for weeks, and sometimes months at a time. At the magazine, she had prestige, security and room for advancement. The weekly paycheck put the roof over her head, the clothes on her back and the food on her table."

"If it hadn't been so important that Lee prove she could do all this for herself, she might have taken the big chance of sending those first hundred pages to a publishing house.

But then...shaking her head, Lee watched the people mill through the registration area, all types, all sizes, all ages, et cetera. Clothes varied from trim, professional business suits to jeans to flamboyant caftans and smocks.

Apparently, style was a matter of taste, and taste a matter of individuality. She wondered if she'd see quite the same variety at any other convention. Absently, she glanced at the partial manuscript she'd tucked into her briefcase. Just for cover, she reminded herself. That was all. "

"No, Lee didn't believe she had it in her to be a Great writer, but she knew she had the skill for great reporting. She'd never, never settle for being second-rate at anything. Still, while she was here, it wouldn't hurt to sit in on one or two of the seminars. She might even pick up some pointers.

More importantly, she told herself as she rose, she might be able to stretch this trip into another story on the ins and outs of a writer's conference. Who attended, why, what they did, what they hoped for. Yes, it could make quite an interesting little piece. The job, after all, came first.

Lee asked "Why are you so secretive about yourself? Most people in your position would make the most of the promotion and publicity that's available." Hunter replied, "I don't consider myself secretive, nor do I consider myself most people." Lee proceeded, "You don't even have a bio or photo on your novel covers.

"Hunter countered again, "My face and my background have nothing to do with the stories I tell." Lee kept going, "Don't you feel it's part of your profession to satisfy the readers curiosity when it comes to the person who creates a story that interests them?"

Hunter parried, "No, my profession is words---putting words together so that someone who reads them is entertained, intrigued and satisfied with my tale. And tales spring from *imagination* rather than hard fact." Lee, "The advice you gave to struggling writers about blocking out time to write every day no matter how discouraged they get---did that come from personal experience?"

Hunter added, "All writers face *discouragement* from time to time. Just as they face criticism *and* rejection." Lee asked then, "Did you face many rejections before the sale of The Devil's Due?" Hunter quipped, "I suspect anything that comes too easily."

Lee, "What made you become a writer?" Hunter, "I was born to be a writer." Lee, "Born to be a writer, do you think that it is really that simple?" Then Hunter responded, "Why yes, yes I do."

(*Citation*: *Second Nature*. Nora Roberts, date unknown).

Note:

If you look closely, very closely, in the next best-selling novel that you read, you will find errors such as I have listed here, and also some others, I always do. Before I was an author I did not notice any errors, I just read for fun, enjoyment and read them very quickly.

I have found out that even the New York Times best sellers make errors, even though they have several very expensive editors.

Now, I hate to admit this to you good readers out there, however, in an effort of full *disclosure*, you will find some of these types of mistakes, or *misspeaks*, as I like to call them, in this said, "How to Write a Novel" self-help book. I wish to apologize up front, as I do not want you to be shocked when you see some of my errors (I like to call them 'faux pas').

You may ask, "Well if you make mistakes, why did you write a book on How to Write a Novel?" My candid answer, if I may give you one, this booklet is not meant to be a perfect example of a novel.

It is meant to *teach* you how to write one. And by the way, you will more than likely have some errors, and or flaws, in you work of art as well.

Finally, if someone does find errors in your novel, and points them out to yourself, do not be defensive, just thank them and tell them that you will correct the mistakes in your next edition of your book. That way you will make a friend, and future reader, instead of making an enemy and losing a reader, right?

CHAPTER SEVEN
SELECT YOUR PUBLISHING MODE

Choose your publishing method before you finish your masterpiece. Your publisher may be able to assist you with lots of questions that you may have, unless you are an experienced author.

Regular Publisher:

This is really not a viable option for you, unless you are a well-known author. First time authors cannot get a professional publisher unless they know them or have some sort of connection. Also due to the bad economy (the Great Recession), over 50% of the publishers have gone bankrupt during the last five years.

The ones that are left, are naturally only doing the already well-established writers. Publishers assist you with covers, text, grammar, spelling, designing, editing as well as many more aspects of writing your literary work of art.

And, by the way, most are only doing eBooks these days, as paperbacks and hard book covers are not selling very well any longer. We have entered the electronic book reading era now and there is no going back, it would appear.

If you do obtain the services of a regular publisher, which as

I said is very unlikely in this day and age, they will require that you sign a legal Contract (Author's Agreement). It will be very long, complicated, as well as confusing. Unless you are an attorney, or have one read it for you.

And you should know that they are now the proud owner of your pride and joy (your novel), and they will now hold all legal Rights to the work (book). They all belong to the Publisher, from now on.

The Agreement will include, the *term* (how long they will own your novel). Normally that would be from two to ten years. You can, and should, however, negotiate the term to close to three years, maximum, if you at all can.

The shorter the term the better for you, of course. Besides the ownership and the terms, the said contract will also include the following sections:

Grant License (copyright).
Term of Author's Agreement.
Termination of Agreement.
How Royalties are paid.
Other Rights (Advertising).
Author Name (pseudonym).
Copyright Law and Ownership.
Previous Publication.
Duplication (for Book Reviews only).
Author's Purchase Discount.
Indemnification of Publisher (of course).
ISBN Number provided.
Termination by Publisher.
Subsequent Works by Author.

Cover Art.
Title Page.
Infringements (author liable, naturally).
Assignment to Others.
Miscellaneous Terms.

Finally, if your publisher wants to require you to purchase 100, or more, copies of your new novel, do not sign the Agreement. A lot of publishers try to take advantage of your burning *desire* to get your masterpiece published.

And they use the agreement as a 'scam' just to cover their out- of-pocket costs as well as make a tidy little profit off of you.

Self- Publisher:

You can get lots of ideas on just how to publish your own literary work by looking on the internet. This is a great way to go if you are quite competent with writing, editing, and computer software. It is very inexpensive as well as a quick way to get your literary work of art on the market.

If you are not, however, a former English or Journalism person, and not that adept with software (like good old me), uploading and downloading PDF and Word documents, you may not do so well with this option. Having said that, it is still the least expensive way to produce your novel for sale, by far.

I have a friend who just self-published a little booklet on meeting people. He is a computer Guru, and also quite good with most all software programs (unlike yours truly). He used to work for IBM back in the day. He did not need a publisher (et cetera) to assist him with his work.

He was able to: write the text, produce a cover (which is not easy, at all), edit, set up his format, and do all of the other many necessary steps to make his booklet complete.

Also, he was able to upload his finished project for sale and marketing. Most of you, I would guess at least, are more like myself, and would not be able to self-publish your Master Piece. And that is quite alright.

If you cannot find a regular publisher, and most likely you will not be able to do that in this day and age, you can take advantage of the wonderful, as well as very easy to use, Amazon or some other co-publisher.

Co-Publisher:

One example of a co-publisher is Amazon (Create Space). They have great software that is very user friendly and they also have extremely excellent customer service for all of their authors. I strongly suggest that you check out this literary publishing option before you choose a different one.

Amazon is a dream come true for a lot of writers, who have spent years trying to find an audience after too many rejection letters to count. And, who also when they were repeatedly told that their novels were no good and would never sell.

Please remember, in the back of your brain, to never stop believing in yourself, never stop trying, **and** of course, never stop writing.

Remember, however, that Amazon (nor any other publisher), can guarantee that your novel will be a number ten best seller, or that it will make, or generate, a large cash flow from the royalties.

They can, and do, however, promise that they will assist you with producing a nice looking, and very professional novel. And, that is saying a lot, in my opinion.

In addition, they will help you market your new book. They will list it on their web site in the USA, Canada, Mexico, Brazil, the UK (England), Germany, France, Spain, Italy, India and Japan. And, it would appear that they will be in many, many other foreign countries within a very few years. They have absolutely wonderful customer (Author) service. Also, it is open 24/7 which is extremely convenient if you are like myself and write/work at night and sleep during the day.

They have dozens, and dozens, of novel covers for you to choose from, also the book set up process is very easy for *first* time writers. They also have an accelerated process for more experienced authors. I have used it before, albeit, I prefer the simple process better. I may have a simple mind, perhaps.

Amazon also will provide you with your needed ISBN (International Standard Book Number) for your novel. Remember that they are a co-publisher (some call them a self-publisher, however, that is not technically correct) and not a regular, ordinary publisher.

Therefore, it is your responsibility (being the author), to produce a complete, well edited, nicely organized, and professional looking book.

Your novel needs to be on a word, or PDF, document to upload to them. You will be required to write the back cover of your novel, the description of your book, (and remember they do not have 'spell check' on the back cover, so make sure that it is correct), plus lots of other supporting information for them to publish your novel and place it on line for sale.

I read this very nice little article from an Amazon/Kindle eBook author. And I would like to share it with you. A nice and also very successful mom who worked full-time while raising four kids, knows all about the publishing *struggle*.

She was able to write a romance novel, but when it came time to publish it, she did not expect a battle that would threaten her whole commitment to writing.

She said her novel took five years to complete, and though she received good feedback from the publishing community in general, no one wanted to publish her book.

With her next two novels, she had the same results. One of them even asked her to add 20,000 more words to her already quite long, novel and then resubmit it to them. She dutifully did that, and she never heard back from them?

She was crushed, to say the least, she thought that finally she had found her publisher. She knew that book 'rejections' were part of the deal of becoming a published author, but she had no idea just how hard it would really be.

All she ever wanted to do, was just get her work in front of some readers. After over 100 rejection letters/emails, there were many days that she thought about quitting altogether.

It felt unfair, somehow, it was like my success was not being based upon my own writing abilities but instead decided by two dozen people in New York City, New York. She knew she deserved better, and that readers would like her books.

Then she discovered a way to take success into her own hands. She learned that any author could publish (co-publish) their Works on Amazon (Create Space) and/or Amazon Kindle eBooks. This could be done by using their independent co-publishing (semi self- publishing), Platform.

After she completed her process with her novel, she expected to sell just a few books. She sold thousands instead. She was thrilled to say the least, naturally. In her first year with Kindle, she sold 250,000 eBooks.

She stated recently that she was just so excited that writers have the opportunity to get their Work in front of readers without jumping through insurmountable hoops by regular publishers. She also noted that the publishing world is changing very fast, and that she planned to "enjoy every minute of the ride."

Note:

This said author (me) received over 125 rejection letters/emails, before finding my first regular publisher. She did publish four (4) mystery novels for me. It did not work out in the long run; however, I learned a great deal about the 'book business.' Then I was very fortunate to find Amazon (Create Space).

I now co-publish (or some would say self-publish) all of my works via them. Including this said little booklet that you are now reading. I also have all of my novels, books, and self-help guides, on Amazon Kindle eBooks as well.

There are lots of co-publishers these days. Previously there were very few and they charged a lot of money to assist you with producing your books, ranging from $5,000.00 to $10,000.00, or more. You can find co-publishers in many various catalogs and they are also listed on the internet as well.

AGENTS:

A successful author recently was quoted as saying that his story was no different from countless other writers. He had completed his first novel and was told that in order to get it published, he would have to obtain the services of a Literary Agent.

This is how it is done, he was told. And that is how it has been for years and years. So, he hit the road, so to speak, looking for one.

Only he found a 'dead end' instead, because very quickly his 'rejection' letters from various agents began to pile up on his desk. He received hundreds of them, from agents whom neither had the time nor the resources to represent a *brand* spanking new author.

It was all about their selling 'units' in a system that was old as well as antiquated. It seemed that his lifelong *dream* of becoming a published author was somehow slipping away. However, he did not give up.

He believed that his book was good and that readers would like it IF only they could see it. Then everything changed, eBooks began a new emerging technology.

From the very start, he saw the great possibilities and their enormous potential. He felt that eBooks would not only change how we read books, but also, what books we read. He heard that anyone (author) can publish their works online, in eBook format. He did, and he has never looked back and is today an extremely successful online writer.

EPILOGUE

Now, in this said author's summary and conclusion ((Epilogue), I wish to make this very important point crystal clear. My little, abbreviated, self-help book on, "How to Write a Novel", is not a "know all and be all' on how to write, format and publish your 'bestselling masterpiece' (at least you and I hope that it will be a great work of art, of course), however, you realize that in this life, there are no guarantee's except 'death *and* taxes'.

Yes, it will assist you greatly, I believe, I truly do. No one gave me this information when I started to write my first mystery crime-fiction genre novel three or four years ago.

I had to gather these key points and ideas and knowledge from dozens and dozens of different sources, the internet, various publishers, other authors, and the good people at Amazon (Create space).

I cannot even begin to count the hours, or months, that I have spent to accumulate this, what I feel is very important as well as very helpful information to save you a lot of the time, hassle, effort, as well as money, like I have spent over the past three or more years.

Please do keep in mind though, please do, that I am not guaranteeing that you will be able to sell a lot of your first books, or that everyone will like what you have written, or even that you will have *no critics*, or that people will say how great your book 'looks'.

What I am stating though, and I do so 'in writing' here, that I am so convinced that my effort will help you at least a little bit (and I hope, a lot), with your dream of becoming a published author. And I feel very strongly that you will like the way your book looks, 'I guarantee it'.

One last point, if I may my good reader, after you have read my effort (book) to assist you with your life long endeavor, and you have finished your first masterpiece, please write and tell me if it helped you.

And after reading my little booklet, I am hoping that someone will write to me and say, "You have a very unique and captivating gift of expressing the Kings English that truly captures and encourages a reader's imagination." Well, I can dream at least, can't I?

Well, just one more last point, I wish to sincerely thank you good readers for purchasing my little self-help book on, "*How to Write a Novel*" in Seven Easy Steps, as well as taking some of your very busy and valuable time to read it, and hopefully try it out. And finally, please feel free to write to myself if you should so desire at:

Dickinson Publishing Corporation
Professor Alan Dale Dickinson
Chairman of the Board and Chief Executive Officer and,
Corporate Vice President and Business Banking Manager
World Corporate Lending Group
BANK OF AMERICA -retired
P.O. Box 3962, Laguna Hills, CA 92654